A+
books

Animal Kingdom

REPTILES

by Janet Riehecky

Consultant: Jackie Gai, DVM
Wildlife Veterinarian

raintree

a Capstone company — publishers for children

Raintree is an imprint of Capstone Global Library Limited, a company incorporated in England and Wales having its registered office at 264 Banbury Road, Oxford, OX2 7DY – Registered company number: 6695582

www.raintree.co.uk
myorders@raintree.co.uk

Edited by Kathryn Clay
Designed by Rick Korab and Juliette Peters
Picture research by Kelly Garvin
Production by Gene Bentdahl
Originated by Capstone Global Library LTD
Printed and bound in China.

ISBN 978 1 4747 3461 5
21 20 19 18 17
10 9 8 7 6 5 4 3 2 1

British Library Cataloguing in Publication Data
A full catalogue record for this book is available from the British Library.

Acknowledgements
We would like to thank the following for permission to reproduce photographs: Alamy/John Cancalosi, 25 (top right); Minden Pictures: Mike Perry, 31 (bottom), Pete Oxford, 30 (tr), Stephen Dalton, 23 (middle); Newscom: Chris Mattison/FLPA/imageBROKER, 23 (tr), Mint Images/Frans Lanting, 22 (m); Science Source/Kenneth M. Highfill, 15 (b); Shutterstock: 108MotionBG, 6 (top left), A Jellema, 9 (b), ACEgan, 28-29, Alex Churilov, 1 (b), Anna Kucherova, 11 (tl), apiguide, 11 (top middle), Arto Hakola, 8 (b), Bill Frische, 18 (tr), BLFootage, 23 (tl), Camilo Torres, 19 (tm), Cathy Keifer, cover (bottom left), ChameleonsEye, 10 (right), choikh, 27 (top), Chokniti Khongchum, 22-23, cosma, 26 (left), Darkdiamond67, 24-25, Davdeka, 16-17, David Havel, back cover, 4 (r), E.O., 19 (tl), Fabien Monteil, 11, Firepac, 29 (t), foryouinf, 13 (b), Girish HC, 10, GUDKOV ANDREY, 31 (t), Heiko Kiera, 5 (t), 12-13, 13 (m), Honey Cloverz, 9 (m), hxdbzxy, 12 (b), Janelle Lugge, 16 (m), Jason Mintzer, 10 (ml), 11 (bm), Jason Patrick Ross, 17 (tl), JASON STEEL, 16 (t), jeep2499, 31 (m), jo Crebbin, 8-9, Joe McDonald, 25 (tl), komkrit Preechachanwate, 6-7, kosmos111, 14-15, Leena Robinson, 7 (b), Marek Velechovsky, 20-21, Matt Cornish, 25 (br), 26-27, Matt Jepson, cover (tl), 10 (t), 12 (t), 25 (bl), Michael Koenig, 6 (b), Mishkin_med, 2-3 (bkg), Mr. SUTTIPON YAKHAM, cover, (tr), Natalila Melnychuk, 22 (b), nattanan726, 1 (tr), Neil Burton, 22 (t), NickEvanKZN, 10 (mr), Nneirda, 19 (tr), Noppharat4569, 13 (t), Omaly Darcia, 32, Ondrej Prosicky, 18-19, Patrick K. Campbell, 30 (b), Philip Yb Studio, cover 1, (bkg), PorKaliver, 19 (b), Poul Riishede, 5 (b), reptiles4all, 7 (tr), 11 (bl), 14 (b), 15 (t), 24 (t), 28 (b), 30 (tl), Rich Carey, 17 (b), Robby Holmwood, 24 (b), Robert Eastman, 15 (m), Rudmer Zwerver, 11 (tr), Rusty Dodson, 11 (br), Sebastian Janicki, 1 (tl), Sergey Uryadnikov, 18 (tl), (m), SibFilm, 6 (tr), Signature Message, 17 (b), Skynavin, 10 (l), Songquan Deng, cover, (br), Sorbis, 4 (l), surassawadee, 28 (t), Stuart G Porter, 20 (b), Suede Chen, 7 (tl), Susan Schmitz, 4-5, Svoboda Pavel, 21, Teri Virbickis, 9 (tr), TongFotoman, 8 (t), Tony Campbell, 17 (tr), Utopia_88, 23 (b), Waclaw Bugno, 18 (b), YapAhock, 9 (tl), Yatra, 29 (b)

Artistic elements: Shutterstock: mishkin_med, nikiteev_konstantin, yyang, Z-art

Every effort has been made to contact copyright holders of material reproduced in this book. Any omissions will be rectified in subsequent printings if notice is given to the publisher.

All the internet addresses (URLs) given in this book were valid at the time of going to press. However, due to the dynamic nature of the internet, some addresses may have changed, or sites may have changed or ceased to exist since publication. While the author and publisher regret any inconvenience this may cause readers, no responsibility for any such changes can be accepted by either the author or the publisher.

CONTENTS

What are reptiles?

Reptiles are a group of animals that have dry, scaly skin or bony plates. Turtles, snakes and lizards are reptiles.

phylum
(FIE-lum)
a group of living things with a similar body plan; reptiles belong to the phylum Chordata (kawr-DEY-tuh); mammals, fish and amphibians are also in this group

kingdom
one of five very large groups into which all living things are placed; the two main kingdoms are plants and animals; reptiles belong to the animal kingdom

class
a smaller group of living things; reptiles are in the class Reptilia

order
a group of living things that is smaller than a class; there are four orders of reptiles

species
(SPEE-sees)
a group of animals that are alike and can produce young with each other; there are more than 10,000 species of reptiles

vertebrate
(VUR-tuh-brut)
an animal that has a backbone; reptiles are vertebrates

amphibian
(am-FI-bee-uhn)
a cold-blooded animal with a backbone, permeable skin and no scales; amphibians are not reptiles

cold-blooded
also called ectothermic
(EK-tuh-THER-mik)
cold-blooded animals have a body temperature that is the same as the air around them; reptiles are cold-blooded

scales
small, hard plates that cover a reptile's body

jaws
the bones of the upper and lower parts of the mouth; jaws hold teeth; saltwater crocodiles have the strongest jaws in the animal kingdom

beak
a sharp, pointy covering on the front of the jaw; turtles and tortoises have beaks

shell
a hard outer covering; shells keep turtles safe

forked
split on the end; snakes and monitor lizards use forked tongues to collect smells from the air

fang
a long, hollow tooth; venomous snakes use fangs to put venom in other animals

claw
a hard, sharp nail on an animal's toe; all reptiles, except snakes and some turtles, have claws

lung
one of two large sacs in the chest that fill with air; reptiles breathe with lungs

dewlap
(DYOO-lap)
a flap of skin that hangs from the neck of some lizards; used to scare enemies, "talk" with other lizards and attract mates

Getting into groups

alligators
large, mostly freshwater reptiles with strong jaws and a rounded nose; the bottom teeth cannot be seen when the jaws are closed

crocodiles
look like alligators, but usually with a pointed nose; the bottom teeth can be seen when the jaws are closed; found in both freshwater and salt water

lizards
have four legs; most have dry, scaly skin

turtles

most have a hard shell into which they can pull their heads and legs; turtles have webbed feet and live mostly in water

tortoises

look like turtles but do not have webbed feet; tortoises live on land

tuataras

(too-uh-TAR-uhs) look like lizards, with two rows of teeth in the upper jaw that overlap a row of teeth in the lower jaw; found only in New Zealand

snakes

do not have legs; a snake's skin is covered in scales

Simply snakes

There are more than 3,000 species of snakes in the world. They come in all sizes, from small garter snakes to giant pythons.

garter snake

a mostly small, colourful snake commonly found in North America; garter snakes may have yellow, green, blue or orange stripes

python

(PYE-thon): a large, non-venomous snake that kills by squeezing; pythons live mostly in Africa and Asia

mamba

a quick, venomous snake that can move faster than a person can run; the black mamba may be the world's deadliest snake

boa

(BOH-uh): a large, non-venomous snake that kills by squeezing; boas live in Central and South America; female boas give birth to live young

cobra

(KOH-bruh): a large, venomous snake that spreads its neck skin to look like a hood

rattlesnake

a venomous snake with thick rings on its tail; rattlesnakes shake their tails as a warning to stay away

Komodo dragon

(kuh-MOH-doh DRA-gun): the largest lizard in the world; Komodo dragons can grow up to 3 metres (10 feet) long and weigh up to 136 kilograms (300 pounds)

Lots of lizards

Think there are a lot of snake species? Lizards outnumber them! There are more than 4,600 species of lizards in the world.

iguana

(ih-GWAH-nuh) a large, green tree-dwelling lizard with a spiny crest on its back

worm lizard

a legless lizard that looks like a snake

chameleon

(kuh-ME-lee-on) a small, tree-dwelling lizard that can change its skin colour to match its surroundings

skink

the largest family of lizards; skinks have smooth, thick bodies and short limbs

gila monster

(HEE-luh mon-ster) a large, venomous lizard

gecko

(GEK-oh): a small, noisy lizard found in the tropics; unlike other lizards, geckos don't have eyelids, so they must lick their eyes clean

Circle of life

egg
most reptiles bury their eggs under ground; reptiles usually hatch in a few weeks, but Komodo dragons take seven to eight months

clutch
a group of eggs; reptile clutch sizes vary from 1 to more than 100 eggs

egg tooth
a sharp bump on top of the head; young reptiles use the egg tooth to break out of their shells

guard
to keep safe; most reptiles leave after laying their eggs, but some skinks, lizards, alligators and crocodiles guard their nests

nest

a structure built by animals to hold their eggs; the king cobra is the only snake that builds a nest for its eggs

hatchling

a young reptile that just came out of its shell; hatchlings look like small adults

live young

babies born directly from their mother, rather than from laid eggs; garter snakes have between five and 100 live young at one time

lifespan

the number of years a certain animal usually lives; the longest living reptiles are Galapagos tortoises (more than 100 years)

life cycle

the series of changes that take place in a living thing, from birth to death

natal beach

(NAY-tuhl BEECH): the place where a sea turtle hatches; sea turtles return to their natal beach to lay eggs of their own

Discovering the world

vibration
(vye-BRAY-shuhn)
a wave of movement;
instead of hearing
sounds, most reptiles
feel vibrations on
the ground

heat pit
a small hole on the
face of some snakes;
heat pits feel heat and
help snakes find food,
even in the dark

sight
chameleons
can move each
eye on its own;
they can look at two
different things at
the same time

Jacobson's organ

two small sacs on the roof of the mouth; snakes and lizards carry smells to the organ with their tongues; Komodo dragons can smell food up to 4 kilometres (2.5 miles) away

touch

snakes feel their surroundings with their tongues

sensory pit

(SEN-suh-ree PIT): a small black speck on the jaws of alligators and crocodiles; sensory pits help animals find food underwater

third eye

tuataras and some lizards have an "eye" on the tops of their heads that helps them sense light and dark

venom
a poisonous substance that can kill or harm another animal; Gila monsters and bearded lizards are venomous

squirt blood
horned lizards can squirt blood out of their eyes; the blood smells bad and can scare away predators

extra skin
to look bigger, cobras spread out the skin on their head and neck, and frilled lizards fan out the skin around their throats

detached tail
the tails of some geckos come off, or detach, if they're grabbed by predators; most will grow back

Endangered!

Many reptiles are endangered. They are at risk of disappearing forever. Some are hunted. Others lose their homes or food sources when people build cities and roads.

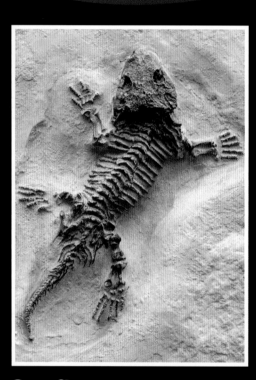

extinct

(ek-STINGKT): no longer living; an extinct animal is one that has died out, with no more of its kind on Earth; dinosaurs are extinct reptiles

endangered

at risk of becoming extinct; Komodo dragons are endangered, numbering fewer than 6,000 in the wild

fossil

(FOSS-suhl): the remains or traces of living things preserved as rock; scientists found a lizard fossil that was 340 million years old

Chinese alligator
the rarest alligator in the world, numbering fewer than 150 in the wild

super croc
also called *Sarcosuchus*; an extinct reptile that lived 110 million years ago; it measured 12 metres (40 feet) long and weighed 9,000 kilograms (10 tons)

poacher
(POH-cher): a person who collects or kills animals illegally; in India more than 10,000 snakes are caught and sold by poachers each month

stegosaurus
a bony-plated dinosaur that fed on plants; stegosaurs had small heads and long, spiky tails

Tyrannosaurus rex
(ti-RAN-uh-sor-uhs REX): a huge carnivore that lived 68 to 66 million years ago; its closest living relatives are birds

27

Reptile records

oldest reptile
a radiated tortoise from Madagascar named Tu'I Malila lived to be nearly 190 years old

smallest reptile
the leaf chameleon of Madagascar measures only 25 millimetres (1 inch) long

longest flight
a flying gecko can glide up to 61 metres (200 feet) from tree to tree

fastest reptile on land
the spiny-tailed iguana can run up to 34 kilometres (21 miles) per hour

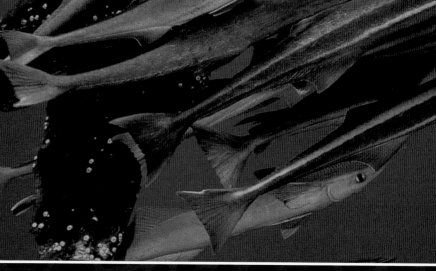

longest wait

tuatara young stay in their eggs for
12 to 15 months before they hatch

heaviest reptile

saltwater crocodiles can weigh
between 400 and 1,000 kilograms
(880 and 2,200 pounds)

fastest swimmer

a leatherback turtle can swim
35 kilometres (22 miles) per hour
for short distances

longest reptile

a python found in Indonesia
in 1912 measured more than
9.8 metres (32 feet) long

Sunlight gives **goldfish** their orange pigment.

Chill out—
KEEP COOL!

Iguanas move into the shade to lower their body temperature.

Moles can tunnel down 90 metres and eat half their body weight in one night.

Bears sleep through the winter, without needing to poo for up to six months.

who
nose!

Every **dog** can be told apart by its unique nose print.

ARMED to the teeth

Sharks have got eight rows of teeth and are always growing new ones, making them dangerous predators. Some sharks will grow up to 80,000 teeth in a lifetime!

KICK UP *your heels*

Kangaroos balance on their tails to kick with both feet.

GO

Monkeys split open bananas from the bottom up – it's easier that way!

Male **monkeys** can go bald – just like humans.

Showering to keep their skin moist is important for an **elephant's** health.

Rats spend a third of their lives washing themselves.

Bees talk to each other by dancing in patterns.

1ST CLASS
SOLDIER

Pigeons have been given medals by the army for delivering messages in dangerous wars.

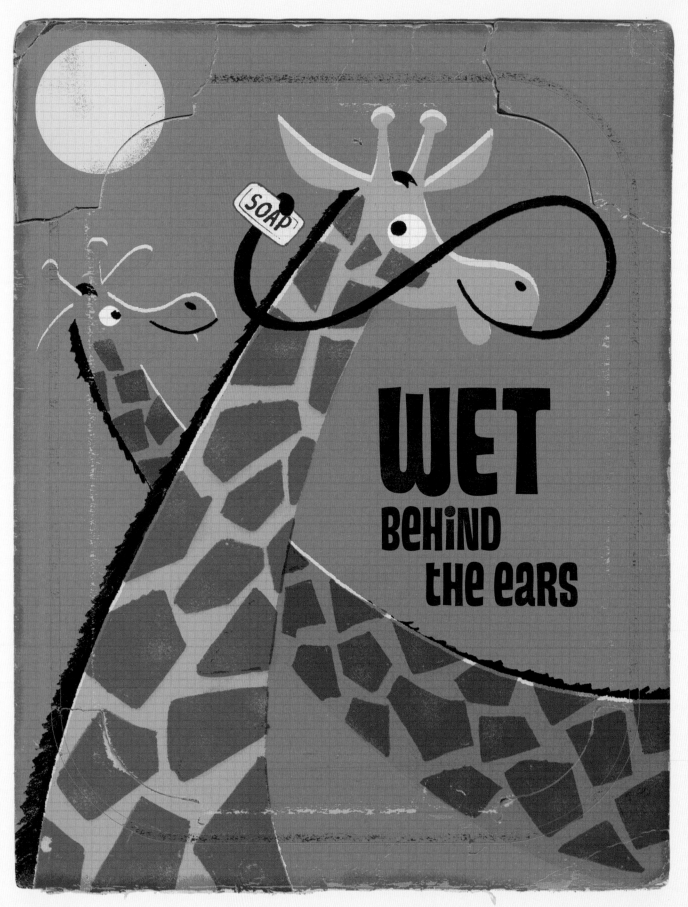

Giraffes use their 50 centimetre tongues to clean themselves all over – including their ears.

Chewing makes **crocodiles'** tear ducts spill watery droplets.

Dolphins sleep with one eye open, resting one half of their brain at a time.

Lions hunt at night, thanks to their ability to see well in the dark.

and **MRS.**

Earthworms can be both male and female – at the same time!

See the LIGHT

Electric eels can produce enough electricity to power ten light bulbs.

Turn a **blind** eye

Rabbits are very short-sighted.

Tigers have amazing binocular vision, which enables them to judge distances when jumping or stalking. Their eyesight is about six times stronger than a human's at night.

Humans may have weaker eyesight, but their intelligence means they can do things that even a tiger cannot – like reading this book!

Originally from Nottingham, now based in London, Paul Thurlby has
been a full-time illustrator since 2006 after graduating from university.

He has built up an impressive list of commissions in editorial,
advertising, publishing and design for clients including the *Guardian*, It's Nice That,
The French Tourist Board, *USA Today*, Orange UK and Warner/Chappell.

He holds his pen in a funny way, but it works just fine for him.

Paul Thurlby's Wildlife is his second book.

For Van, Becca, Gabriel, Lottie and Imogen.

A TEMPLAR BOOK

First published in the UK in 2013 by Templar Publishing,
an imprint of The Templar Company Limited,
Deepdene Lodge, Deepdene Avenue, Dorking, Surrey, RH5 4AT, UK
www.templarco.co.uk

ISBN 978-1-84877-858-0

Edited by Jenny Broom

Printed in China